Puppy Training

A Step-by-Step Guide to Crate Training, Potty Training, and Obedience Training

Alexa Parsons

Table of Contents

Introduction

Once you have found the perfect puppy to join your family, you need to make sure your new friend is properly trained. Training your puppy will help him understand what is expected of him and enable him to gain confidence. Proper training will also strengthen the bond between you and your puppy, and make it possible for you to include your puppy in your daily activities more often. A well-trained puppy is a happy, well balanced puppy, and of course, that's what you want for your new best friend.

There are different theories about how to train a puppy. Some people believe in firmness and strict commands. Others tell you that providing rewards for good behavior and taking away rewards for bad behavior is essential. The best course of action will depend on your dog's personality.

This book will make puppy training a whole lot easier for you. It features proven methods and step-by-step instructions for training your puppy and introducing him to your home, your visitors, and the general public. Chapter 1 helps you understand your puppy and his personality, Chapter 2 provides you with useful puppy training tips, and Chapter 3 explains crate training. Potty training is one of the most important tasks to teach your puppy when he comes home, and Chapter 4 covers it in depth. In addition, Chapter 5 introduces the best way to teach him obedience commands, Chapter 6 introduces clicker training, and Chapter 7 shows you how to walk your puppy. Finally, Chapter 8 contains key tips on how to stop destructive behaviors.

While it may seem daunting to teach a new puppy everything he needs to know, the truth is that puppies are usually very eager to please their new families. When training your new puppy, you're bound to make mistakes, and your pet will too. With patience and consistency, your puppy will learn what he is supposed to do and you will be well on your way to building an extremely satisfying, lifelong friendship that will be more rewarding than you ever thought possible.

Chapter 1: Understanding Your Puppy

If you want to train your puppy properly, you need to understand what is causing him to act the way he does. You have to understand his psychology, and you'll be surprised to learn how much he resembles a child. It's your job to read the behavior of your puppy and adjust the training accordingly.

Dog Psychology

Think of your dog as an infant that will grow quickly. He is born with certain instincts, but this won't teach him what he needs to know in order to become a beloved member of your household. The puppy's mother will use imprints on his memory to teach him, and you'll have to learn to do the same. You'll need to teach him to smell certain things to tell if the smell is good or bad, and you'll need to use imitation as well. It's important for him to imitate you. For example, if you bark then he will bark.

If you always turn electronics, such as the TV, off at night, then your puppy will learn that these lights being turned off mean that it's bed time. Your puppy will learn these routines through your habits, which is where consistency comes in handy. Associate learning is another process that you'll need to teach your dog. Associate learning is tying a motivational reason or a reward to the training. He is motivated by instinct, which makes him want love, shelter, food and water.

A puppy has needs and desires that as an owner, you're supposed to meet. You have to teach your puppy appropriate actions and ignore any inappropriate behavior. If you give your puppy attention for his negative behavior, then he will start to associate that behavior with the ability to get your attention. Keep in mind that your puppy has emotions. He can be fearful, bored, worried, happy, sad and even depressed. It's up to you to be able to interpret these feelings.

Puppy's Personality

A puppy will start to develop his personality at about seven weeks. His full personality can usually be seen at ten to twelve weeks. If you want to choose a puppy based on his personality, it's important to wait at least seven weeks. You should visit your puppy before finalizing your choice at ten to twelve weeks to check on his personality again.

Keep in mind that the environment that he is being kept in can affect his personality. Your puppy may act differently where he was born versus your home. Genetics will also factor into your puppy's personality. Different breeds have different traits, so it's important that you read up on dog breeds before you pick one.

Chapter 2: Puppy Training Tips

Puppies are naturally playful, curious and active. Those traits are going to be fun most of the time, but in order to keep your friend safe and protected, you want to help him establish boundaries. The best tip to start with is that you have to think about your puppy like you would a human child. Treat him as if he were an infant or a toddler. Here are some puppy training tips that you can use to teach your puppy everything he needs to know to start the journey of becoming your best friend.

Puppy Proofing Your Home

One of the first things you will need to do with a new puppy is to puppy-proof your home. Set up gates and close doors, keeping the puppy confined to a specific space. Your little dog is probably not housebroken yet, and you don't want to clean up messes all throughout your home. Keeping the puppy within your range of sight for the first few weeks is essential. You'll also want to pick up anything that's on the ground. Puppies are famous for chewing up clothes, shoes, your child's favorite toy and anything else they can get their eager little mouths around.

Choosing a Collar

A collar is a functional accessory that your dog will wear around his neck. The collar can attach to a leash or a harness when it's time to go for a walk and it can also be used to hold any dog tags or documentation that you received when you registered your puppy. There are collars on the market that can also be used to train your dog and instill good behaviors.

When you are gathering your supplies, buy items that can grow with your puppy. Collars should be adjustable and checked frequently for a proper fit. Puppies grow quickly and you do not want the collar to be too tight or uncomfortable. When fitting your puppy's collar, be sure that you can fit two fingers between the collar and his neck. This measurement will help ensure the collar is snug enough to keep your puppy secure, but won't be tight and uncomfortable. If your puppy starts to scratch at his collar, distract him with a toy, treat or with verbal distractions to take his mind off it. When you're shopping for collars, make sure the collar you select has a sturdy metal ring to attach the leash to when you begin to leash train and walk your puppy.

Habits start in puppyhood, so you want to make sure you're reinforcing good behavior and punishing bad behavior. It's never too early to start. If you've got a bit of a barker on your hands, you can find a collar that discourages barking. Choose a chain collar for stubborn pups who are tempted to take off or refuse to move when they need to.

Choosing a Leash

The leash accompanies the collar, especially if you don't have an outdoor space where your puppy can run free. It might seem like walking on a leash should be second nature to your puppy, but it's actually a learned behavior.

Look for a leash that is secure and fits well on the collar or the harness you're using. When selecting the first leash to use for your puppy, pick one that is lightweight. A heavy leash may add pressure to the puppy's neck and make leash training more difficult than it needs to be. Give the puppy enough leash space to roam around independently, but not so much leash that the dog can run into traffic or get into trouble. Retractable leashes are often a good option because you can decide how much freedom you want to give your little buddy.

Crate Training

Another type of training tool that dog owners find useful is the crate. A dog crate is like a cage where dogs can sleep and spend time when you're out of the house. This protects your property by keeping your puppy from destroying your house while you are unable to supervise him. It's also a way for your new puppy to feel safe. While there might be some whimpering and resistance the first time you confine your pup to a crate, the training will work quickly and your dog will become accustomed to the security of it.

When shopping for a crate, look for crates just large enough for your puppy to stand and turn around in. If your puppy will soon grow too large for a crate, look for larger crates that include a crate divider. This way, you can use the crate divider to block off half the crate until your puppy grows large enough to fill the crate space and you avoid the expense of buying multiple crates. Put the crate in your bedroom at night if your dog has separation anxiety. Many people also find that placing an article of their clothing or an old towel inside the crate is a good idea; the dog will be comforted by your scent.

Treats and Rewards

Everyone, including puppies, loves treats. You can use these as a reward for good behavior. Dog treats come in all flavors, sizes and specialties. Soft, meaty treats are very enticing to most puppies, and having a ready supply on hand will help your puppy quickly learn what behaviors are wanted and rewarded. Puppies usually love treats with cheese, peanut butter or meat flavor. Select small treats instead of big ones that require a lot of chewing. The trick with training is to use quick, positive reinforcement and small, bite-sized treats as a perfect reward for your puppy.

Drop a treat into the crate in order to lure your dog inside. Provide a treat anytime the puppy goes to the bathroom outside or sits and rolls over when commanded. Don't give your dog treats for no reason, or this will confuse the situation and he won't realize he's being rewarded. Make sure it is a suitable dog treat that you're providing as well.

Your rewards should also vary. If you always give him a treat following a voice command, he will associate the command with food. If he doesn't want or need food, then he'll refuse the command. Instead, if your rewards include giving him a treat, soothing him, playing with him, or petting him, then he knows that he will get some type of reward when following the command. This way a puppy will learn to always listen to his commands.

Communicating Your Intentions Clearly

There's nothing wrong with explicitly telling your puppy "no", only that it often fails to offer enough information. Instead, you can tell him what you want. Dogs don't usually generalize well, so if the dog jumps on someone in excitement and you say "no", he may jump higher or change direction. A better alternative would be to instruct him to sit. Telling him what you want helps avoid confusion.

One of the biggest mistakes when trying to use voice commands is to use too many words. Your dog can associate words, but it takes some time. You'll want a word that is to the point. Finish learning one command before moving on to another. If you move on to other commands too quickly, then your dog may get confused.

Be Consistent

You have to be consistent if you want your puppy to be consistent. You can't work for an hour on a sit command and then just not take up his training again for a week or two. You have to work on the same command until he gets it right.

Establish routines with your puppy, such as regular feeding times, walk, and play times, and bathroom breaks. Stick with your routines and this will help speed up the process. It's not just about training commands either. A routine for your puppy will help him get up when you do, play when you feel up to it, and eat when you are able to feed him. This way you aren't rearranging your schedule to take care of your puppy. Instead, you'll be teaching him to work on your schedule so that he works with you.

If you don't want your puppy to jump on people when they come through the front door, you need to reinforce that expectation every time. Allowing the pup to jump all over your sister, but not your neighbor will cause confusion. Use the "sit" or "stay" or "heel" command to get your puppy's attention and do it every time. Be consistent since inconsistencies will only confuse him and prolong the training process.

Use Repetition

Repetition is key in dog training. For example, ask your dog to sit and give him a treat for the first two times. For the third time, try a different type of reward, such as petting and praise. This will teach him that he gets rewarded in different ways by listening to your commands, and this type of repetition can be extremely useful in training your puppy.

Be Patient

Don't allow yourself to get frustrated or impatient during the training process – either with yourself or with your new puppy. It will take some time to accomplish all the goals you have set for your new pal and for you to get the hang of your puppy's unique personality, likes, and the techniques and rewards that work best for your puppy.

Give your puppy time to understand new commands. He most likely won't learn it the first couple of times when you teach him. Repeat old commands in new training sessions, so that he doesn't forget them. The attention span of a dog is pretty short, so keep your sessions frequent but short in duration, otherwise your pup will become bored.

Never get impatient with your puppy and never call him to you if you are going to punish him – all that will do is teach him that coming to you is not a good thing. Keep your voice firm but gentle, and never let any frustration creep into it.

Training Yourself

When you introduce a new dog into your household and your life, you're not just training the puppy. You're training yourself as well. Your life is going to have to change, and you need to be prepared for it and willing to adapt. Sleeping in until noon on the weekends is no longer an option when you have a puppy that needs to be walked and fed. Taking off for a spontaneous vacation sounds like fun, but first you'll have to make arrangements for the pup. Working with the dog to be calm and quiet when friends and family visit takes a lot of energy and a willingness to hang in there for the long term.

You are working on forming a lifelong bond. Be patient and consistent with the process and it will work. All the puppy training tips in the world won't work if you have a short fuse or lack interest in making your puppy comfortable and well behaved. Puppies are adorable, but they're also a lot of work. Before you take the plunge into new puppy ownership, make sure you're willing to invest the time, emotional energy and resources. For specific puppy training tips, you can call on experts in the field. Pet stores, veterinarians and fellow dog owners can all help you and your puppy become good roommates and family members.

Chapter 3: Crate Training for Puppy

It might seem cruel–the idea of confining a dog to a metal crate. However, crates make puppies feel safe and secure as they mimic the dog's natural den habitat. Crate training your puppy is an excellent idea, especially if you want your dog to sleep in the crate at night or you plan to be out of the house for most of the day.

Creating a Den

Prepare the crate by making sure it's clean and in a quiet, private area of the house. Dogs like a view, so if you have a nice window next to which you can place the crate - even better. Some people like to put a toy or a blanket in the crate for a puppy. This is a great idea, but if your dog is prone to chewing things to shreds, you might want to wait until you have that behavior modified. Puppies need a den that is clear of debris. Crates come in a number of different sizes, and you can find crates that are metal, plastic and even fabric.

Crate Training Steps

You have to introduce the crate slowly, and make sure you do it in a casual manner. You can't just bring your puppy home and then throw him in a crate. You certainly can't just lock him inside of it. You have to make the crate seem like it's a casual piece of furniture in your home.

First, introduce your dog to the crate. Some puppies will immediately be curious and might even start to explore the crate, walking in and out freely. If your puppy isn't that curious or relaxed, sit next to the crate and encourage your dog to come to you. Keep your tone and your voice happy and positive. Keep the crate door open, but not so loose that it can swing shut or scare the puppy.

Drop some small treats into the crate to encourage your puppy to go in there alone. If the dog doesn't want to go all the way in, don't force him. Give him time to understand that it's safe and to chase those treats. Some people have had success by feeding their puppies meals in the crate. Place a small bowl of food and water in there and see if your pup is willing to enter. This is especially useful if you'll be leaving the house for work every day. It's important your puppy eats and drinks without defecating in the same place because he is going to be there all day. This will help him to try to control his bladder.

Once your puppy is comfortable going in and out of the crate (which could take a few days), begin closing the door of the crate. Sit next to the crate for 10 or 20 minutes the first time you do this. Once your puppy relaxes, get up and leave the room. You might hear barking or whining, and that's okay. Come back into the room after about 10 minutes and sit next to the crate again. Then, let the puppy out. Keep repeating this until you are able to leave the room without your puppy barking.

You don't want to teach your puppy that barking or whining is going to get him out of the crate. The whining should stop before you open the door. If you open the door immediately, he'll start to associate whining as the way to get you to open the door. The behavior will only increase. Although, you need to be careful that you don't create stress in your puppy either. You should increase the time your puppy stays in the crate gradually.

When you and your puppy get to the point that entering the crate is not a struggle and you can be in another room for half an hour without any barking or begging, you can probably leave the house and safely keep your puppy in the crate. Try not to be gone too long. Puppies don't have the bladder strength of older dogs, and they will need to go outside every few hours.

For Nighttime

You'll want to make this a part of your puppy's daily routine. If you want a dog to sleep in a crate, you need to get him started with that schedule from the first day. Your puppy is going to whine at first, but you should ignore him and maybe keep the lights on low. Your puppy will start to associate quietness and darkness with bedtime, so he'll know to stop whining.

You'll have to be patient until you get your puppy to that point. However, if your dog doesn't stop whining in a week you'll want to find a room where there isn't anything to destroy and no stimulation. Close the door, leave the crate open inside of it, and let your puppy associate this with his routine. They'll likely sleep in the crate at night. Many puppies just want the offer of freedom which a closed crate does not allow for.

One thing you should never do is use the crate as a punishment. Don't put your puppy in there as a retaliation for misbehaving, barking or biting. Crate training requires a feeling of comfort and security for your pup.

All dogs are different. You might have a puppy who loves the crate or you might have a puppy who needs constant treats as bribes to get into the crate. If your puppy associates the crate with a safe place, you'll eventually be able to tell when he is feeling stressed, insecure or sick by watching how often he goes into the crate.

Chapter 4: Housebreaking Your Puppy

For many people, potty training their puppy is the most daunting part of bringing a new puppy into the family. Potty training a puppy can be time consuming and messy. However, it's absolutely essential for your dog's growth and development, as well as your peace of mind.

You'll want to mark out a clear space to house break him. One of the best things to use is a puppy pad, and many have fragrances to help avoid the ammonia smell in your home. If your dog doesn't go on the pad, even when he is trained, instead of thinking you have a bad dog, you'll want to consider that he doesn't like the smell of the pad. It may smell amazing to you, but it may irritate his overly sensitive nose.

Step by Step

This section will provide you with a step by step guide on how to housetrain your puppy.

1. Clear the Room: You need to start by clearing the room so that your dog isn't confused by anything. A playpen will sometimes work if you have a small breed, but never use a closet. You don't want your dog to feel like you don't love him and are punishing him. A storage room will help, and so will a spare bedroom.

2. Plastic: Put some plastic on the floor to protect your flooring.

3. Newspaper: Next, you're going to cover the plastic with newspaper because it is easier to clean.

4. Puppy Pads: You'll then place two or three puppy pads in the room.

5. Sleeping Space: You'll need to have a puppy bed or a crate, so that your puppy has a designated sleeping space in the same room.

6. Food & Water: Your new puppy will be spending a lot of time here, so make sure that you have a dedicated area for food and water that your dog can get used to as well.

7. Pay Attention: You have to pay attention for signs of when your dog needs to relieve himself. When he starts to show these signs, you have to carry him to the puppy pad. He doesn't know to go to it yet, so this is your responsibility as his owner.

8. Be Persistent: When your puppy tries to walk away or starts to sniff another area, pick him up and place him back on the pad. Make sure to do this gently and calmly so that you're correcting the behavior but not punishing him.

9. Provide Treats: Once your dog goes on the pad, you need to reward him with a treat immediately.

10. Keep repeating: You'll need to keep repeating all of this so that he understands he should potty on the pads.

The age of your puppy determines just how frequently he has to use the bathroom. Make sure you clean up any space that's been soiled, so he won't attempt to go there again. You need to remove the odor, which is one reason that you put the plastic down in order to make your job easier. You can then start to provide a clean pad each and every time for your puppy.

For Outside Bathrooms

If you don't want to have him going in the house, you'll want to train him to go outside. You have to choose the rules on where you want him to do his business, so it's important that you train him to go inside or outside early on. Outside takes a little more dedication, and here are the steps to train your puppy.

1. Every Hour: You need to start by taking your puppy out each and every hour, making sure to go with him. You will need to take your puppy out immediately after he wakes up, 15 minutes after he eats or drinks, at least once an hour while he is awake, before you put him in his crate and immediately after you take him out of the crate. To help prevent accidents, be sure you keep your puppy on a regular feeding schedule and remove the food once he has finished eating, but always allow him access to water. Your puppy's digestive system is quick and efficient, and taking him out 15 minutes after he eats will help get him used to going potty outside.

Puppies cannot be expected to hold their bladders all night, so you will also need to set an alarm during the night so you can take him outside. Expecting your puppy to hold his bladder throughout the night is not only unrealistic, it is a sure fire way to ensure he soils his crate or gets a bladder infection trying to hold it far longer than he is capable of or should be expected to. It is also important to watch for bathroom "tells" puppies often display. Twirling in circles, whining, scratching and sniffing the floor are often indications the puppy needs to potty, so if you see or hear these things, take him outside immediately.

2. Call Him: You can call him by name or put a leash on him to have him follow you. Be consistent on which you use.

3. Pick an Area: You can pick a spot and train him like you would with a puppy pad. It is important that you take your puppy to the same spot every time to use the bathroom. Your dog will be able to sniff the area and tell where he went to the bathroom before. Be patient with your puppy, do not try to force him, yell at him or rush him to use the potty. Simply stand in the designated spot and use upbeat, positive verbal encouragements to "go potty" and allow your puppy time to sniff out the perfect spot and relieve himself. Once your puppy does his business, be sure to reward him with positive praise, a treat, and a lot of snuggles, pets and kisses. Make it a rewarding, happy experience so your dog feels good when he sees you get the leash and say the words "go potty". Most puppies truly want to please their masters and letting your puppy know he is good and did the right thing will help your puppy's potty training progress at a faster rate.

If He Doesn't Listen

If your dog doesn't listen, then you need to provide more training. Pay attention to what he likes. Does he like praise more than treats? Are you making sure to vary it? You should have started off with treats and progressed to praise. Also, you could be trying to rush your puppy. If you rush him, then he won't go in the right area because he feels the need to hurry. Puppies can pick up on your impatience, so try to calm down. Puppies less than 12-16 weeks old simply do not have enough control over their bladders to be potty trained. Hold off on outside potty training until your puppy is at least 12 weeks old.

How to Handle Accidents

Accidents are going to happen. Sometimes when a young puppy gets excited, he can accidently use the bathroom without meaning to. Just accept accidents as part of the process and do not overreact to them. Your puppy is not being willful, disobedient or resistant. It's simply part of the process, so do not punish him by spanking him, rubbing his nose in it or yelling at him. If you notice your pup is beginning to pee or poop in the house, clap your hands or make a loud noise. You want to startle the puppy and get its attention, but you don't want to scare him. Calmly say "No" and take him to his spot outside.

When an accident does occur in the house, simply clean it up and move on. You cannot apply a correction after the fact –

the puppy will have no idea what is going on, why he is being told "No" or what he was supposed to do. Unlike us, puppies live in the moment and once it has passed, they do not have a recollection of the accident, so trying to discipline a puppy for a past action will only make him scared and make it difficult for him to trust you. Never, ever strike your puppy when you find accidents, or for any other reason. Hitting your puppy will only crush his spirit and break the bond you are trying to build; it will not correct his behavior or make the process faster.

Be patient and consistent with your potty training routine and be gentle, kind and loving with your puppy. You'd never yell at, punish or berate a baby for accidents, so don't do it to your puppy. Follow these potty training tips and in just a few weeks, your puppy will be potty trained and you can feel good about a job well done.

Chapter 5: Obedience Training

There are many different theories about how to train a puppy. Some people believe in firmness and strict commands that come with consequences. Other schools of thought will tell you that providing rewards for good behavior and taking away rewards with bad behavior is the best way to train a puppy. The best course of action really depends on your dog and the animal's specific personality. Some puppies will be interested in pleasing you and others will not really care what you think. The best way to approach obedience training with your puppy is to use consistent practice. Remember that puppies are young and active, so keep your training sessions short and make sure they are not hungry or tired.

Obedience Training: Teaching to Heel

Teaching your puppy how to heel is important, especially when there are other dogs around, or people that your dog might want to jump on without invitation. When you command your dog to heel, the dog will sit by your side quietly until released. This is a difficult thing for puppies to learn, especially since they are so energetic and curious by nature.

The key to this part of puppy training is of course treats. Start by standing with your puppy on a leash and keep a few treats in the hand that isn't holding the leash. The puppy needs to understand the command, so tell your dog to heel. Once he sits still next to you for about five seconds, give the dog a treat. Then, take five steps forward and allow your dog to follow. Say the word "heel" and wait for your puppy to sit down next to you. Reward with a treat. Continue doing this so your puppy understands. The dog will associate your movements and words with the expected behaviors.

Once this is successfully completed in the same location, introduce some other people and distractions. You might feel like you're starting the process all over again, but that's only because your puppy will notice those other people or bouncing balls or moving cars. Repeat the process with the treats until your dog is obedient and able to heel on command.

Obedience Training: Teaching to Sit

Teaching your puppy to sit is not complicated, and the dog will understand what you want when you reward with treats and physically show the animal what you expect. Stand in front of your puppy and hold your hand above his head with a treat in it. He will look up at it. Use your other hand to gently push down on his hind quarters until he's in a sitting position. At the same time, while still holding the treat, say "sit" in a calm but firm voice. Once he is able to hold the position, give the puppy the treat. Keep repeating this action until the puppy is able to put himself into a sitting position without your guidance. Ultimately, the pup will be able to sit without your help. This is especially useful for greeting situations when you're introducing your dog to new people. Tell the puppy to sit and when that happens, be forthcoming with the treat.

If your puppy temporarily loses the training you've mastered, simply start again. You might notice your puppy jumps on people when they come into your house or runs after children in the neighborhood. Give the command to sit, and if the dog does not listen, go back to the basics with the treat and the physical lowering of your dog into the sitting position.

Obedience Training: Teaching to Stay

Teaching a puppy to stay is difficult because it's counter-intuitive to a puppy, who wants to explore and jump and sniff and bark. First, designate a spot where you want your dog to stay. That might be a dog bed, a corner of the room or a particular place that keeps the puppy away from whatever you're doing. Give the command to "stay" and use your hand to tell the puppy where you want him to go. You can pat a space on the floor or the sofa next to you, or you can point to a particular spot on the floor with your hand. Continue to repeat the word "stay" so your puppy knows to associate that word with the command. Praise the puppy when you get the obedience you're looking for and the dog goes to the spot you have designated. Wait 10 seconds and reward your pup with a treat.

Obedience Training: Teaching to Come

Puppies always want to come when they're called. They want to know what you're up to and they're going to be eager to be close to you and be a part of whatever you're doing. However, it can be difficult to get your puppy to come if the dog is preoccupied with something else. Maybe the puppy is digging in the backyard or stalking a squirrel or completely obsessed with the scent on some random car's tires. The trick is to teach the dog that coming to you is the best decision that could ever be made. When you call your puppy's name and your little buddy comes running over, shower that dog with praise and love and treats. With that kind of affection and positive reinforcement, your puppy will never want to miss the opportunity to come to you when called.

For training purposes, call your puppy from one room to another. Stand in the kitchen, when your puppy is in the living room, and call the dog by name. When your puppy comes running, get excited, pet him and provide a treat. When the puppy is able to understand that coming when called means only positive things, he will obey immediately.

Obedience Training: Teaching to Lie Down

Training your puppy to lie down is similar to the way you trained the dog to sit. Find a spot that you want the dog to associate with lying down. That will likely be a dog bed or a mat. Pat the place with your hand and say the words "lie down." If you need to, lower your dog's body to the floor so the puppy understands what lying down means. Reward the final act with a treat. Keep practicing until your puppy gets it. Your puppy might have some of his own ideas about where the best places to lie down are. Respect that instinct and train the pup to lie down in the places that he seems most comfortable.

Obedience Training: Teaching "No"

Puppies don't know right from wrong and if you want them to stop chewing, biting, jumping or barking, you need to train them to understand the word "no." When your puppy does something you don't like, say the word "no" in a firm, loud voice. You only want to say it once because you're training the dog to listen the first time. If the puppy obeys, reward with a treat. Redirect the puppy to something else. For example, if he is chewing on a piece of clothing, give him a toy. Again, consistency and patience are absolutely required. You won't be able to train your new puppy overnight. However, with time and structure, obedience training can be conquered.

Chapter 6: Clicker Training

For many puppies, a clicker is a great way to train them. Small and inexpensive, clickers work by capturing your dog's attention with an audible sound. You'll use the clicker with a voice command, and if they do the right thing then you'll give your puppy a treat.

Benefits of a Clicker

This method helps to stop your dog from being dependent on the treats and still listen to you. You won't have to call or yell at your puppy, and he can hear the clicker at a long range. This makes it easier to train him to your voice, and your puppy will start to look to you for leadership more quickly.

Simply press the clicker's button when your puppy does what you want him to do and follow the click with a positive reward, such as a small treat or an enthusiastic, encouraging pet, a scratch behind the ears and a "good boy/girl!" verbal reinforcement.

Step by Step

Here is a step by step on how to train your dog using a clicker. Make sure you get a clicker that works well to get started.

1. Use a Command: You have to start off with a goal in mind. What behavior do you want to target first? One of the best ones to target is "sit". Raise your hand up with a treat visible in it and tell your puppy to sit.

2. Treat: Make sure that you give the treat once he is in the right position. You don't want to have too long of a delay or this will hurt the association process.

3. Repeat: Do it all over again, and make sure that you use the same movement along with the same tone.

4. Vary Reward: Do it a few more times, and once you do you'll need to vary the reward you're giving him. Sometimes just pet him, sometimes say "good boy/girl!" and sometimes use the treat.

5. Clicker: Once the puppy has already made the association, that's when the clicker comes in. Repeat the process of asking him to sit, then press the clicker's button, and follow the click with a positive reward, such as a small treat or an encouraging pet. He doesn't know what the new noise is yet.

6. Repeat: This time you're going to tell your dog to sit, holding the clicker and treat over his head. Remember to click it as you lift it up. Give him a treat. Keep repeating.

7. Clicker: Use just the clicker, and if you dog sits give him a treat. You don't have to use words now.

Make sure that you never train your dog in a way where the clicker just gets his attention. You need to assign it to a certain command. Keep in mind that some dogs will learn slower than others, and you can't expect your puppy to learn to respond to the clicker in just a day or two. When you teach your dog another command with the clicker, then you need to vary the clicking. One click may be "sit", but two rapid clicks will need to be something like "lie down". However, if you want to add another such as "stay," you can use either three rapid clicks or two slow clicks. If you have a hard time with your puppy not wanting to listen, try giving him a break. Just like kids, he sometimes needs to go out for recess, and school can't be every single day.

Chapter 7: Going for Walks

Your puppy needs exercise and fresh air to help him stay calm, grow healthy and get the stimulation he needs to stave off boredom and the destructive behaviors that often accompany boredom. While playing with your puppy is fun and provides some exercise, walking your puppy is the best way to help him expend pent up energy and calm his mind. Once your puppy is leash trained, walking him is an enjoyable way for the two of you to bond and provides you with time to clear your mind and get some exercise, too.

The Normal Puppy

An untrained puppy isn't aware of the dangers around him. He will strain against his leash, and he'll hate that he can't get free. He'll buck, jump, and do anything he can to get out of his harness or collar. He'll also want to stop and smell everything he can. A puppy gets a lot of information from his sense of smell, and he can tell if something is good or bad, if another animal has been around, or even if it's just interesting to him. He will often forget he's on a leash at all, and he may wrap around you if you aren't careful. He may try to run ahead and pull you with him if he can. The following leash training tips will have you proudly walking a well behaved, happy pup sooner than you ever thought possible.

Introduce the Collar

There are dozens of different collar and leash styles to choose from, and the best one for you will depend on your dog. Small dogs do well in a harness so they can't slip out of their collars. That works well for puppies of all breeds.

When you first introduce the collar to your pup, be sure it fits properly. There should be enough room for you to fit two fingers between the collar and your pup's neck. Make putting the collar on fun by using an upbeat, but calm voice and reward your pup with a treat once the collar is fastened. Some puppies will try to push the collar off or scratch at it; after all, it is a new sensation. If your pup does this, distract him with a toy, a treat or scratching behind his ears. Anytime you see your pup messing with his collar, apply a positive distraction and soon your puppy won't even notice he's wearing a collar.

Introduce the Leash

Once your puppy is used to the collar, it's time to introduce him to the leash. Select a lightweight leash so there is no unnecessary pulling that may make your puppy leery of the leash. Clip the leash onto the collar and call your puppy to you. Some puppies will have a major reaction to the leash and thrash around wildly trying to get it off. This is normal, so simply drop the leash and allow your puppy to pull it behind him as he wriggles, squirms and hops. Do not let your puppy out of your sight since the leash can become caught up on something and hurt him. Continue to put the leash on for short periods of time, dropping down to one knee and calling your puppy to you with a reward when he comes. Once he reaches you, pick up the leash and walk him short distances around the house. Repeat this a couple of times a day until your puppy is accustomed to the leash. Make the process fun by verbally praising your puppy and offering treats. If he tries to bite leash, remember to tell him "No." Never let your puppy treat his leash like a toy.

After your puppy understands the sit and stay commands, you can teach him the "walk" command. You can do this with or without the clicker. Walk to your puppy, and say "walk" while you start walking. You should give him a treat if he walks in the same direction as you. You then ask him to sit and then stay, and remember to praise good behavior. You'll need to repeat this process until he starts to associate the word "walk" with the movement you're making.

Never pull or tug harshly on the leash, fight your puppy on the leash or yell at your puppy as those negative behaviors will only confuse the puppy and set your training back. Be patient with your pup and keep a consistent routine of attaching the leash and letting your pup get used to it slowly and at his own pace.

His First Walk

By now, your puppy is used to walking short distances inside the house on a leash and it's time to take the fun outside. The outside world offers a lot of fun and distraction, so even though your pup knows how to be led on the leash, he may act differently outside.

Go to the door and when your puppy follows, you'll need to tell him to sit and stay. Then you're going to put the harness or collar and leash on, finally opening the door. If the puppy reaches the end of his leash, then tell him to sit and stay. If he shows improper behavior due to excitement, just ignore it. Give him a treat when he follows the commands.

If he pulls, stop, stand completely still, and do not move until he comes back to you. If he is becoming too much to handle, always try the sit and stay command instead of pulling or shortening the leash he's on. Let your dog smell things, use the bathroom, have fun, and walk around the space with you. Be patient. Start with short walks at first and soon you and your pup can increase the time and distance.

Just make sure that you stay in the leadership role, and then repeat the process with different rewards. He'll start to eventually associate his collar or harness as well as the leash with walking with you, which will make him excited. You can start to add new commands as you test new boundaries with your puppy. For example, if you put the leash on the left, then you can teach him to turn left.

If you have it on the right, then he can learn to turn right. When it's just straight above him, then your puppy will know to keep walking straight. If you want to teach your dog to eventually walk without a leash, you can start by teaching him hand signals. When he starts listening to how to walk, then he is ready for trails, dog parks and other new places.

If He Sees Another Dog

Your dog is bound to get excited with his new adventures. If your puppy sees another dog, he is likely to want to rush up to them. He might want to do this if he sees another person too, which means he could forget the commands that you taught him. You'll have to remind him that he listens to you by tightening or shortening the leash a little. This will pull your puppy right towards you, which will limit his ability to pull away or jump.

Tell your puppy to sit and repeat the command, and then tell him to stay. Reward him if he exhibits proper behavior. It can take several tries to get them to calm down, but this is essential to training a puppy properly. This is why it's important to have treats with you when you take your puppy on walks. Most of the time, telling him he's good and petting him is enough, but sometimes a treat is needed or just wanted. Food is one of your most powerful motivators, but make sure that you change where you keep the treats on you. You don't want your puppy to just start listening because he sees you going for a treat.

The Length of Walks

You may be wondering how long your puppy should be on his walk, and this is based on different factors. Keep in mind how warm it is, how much stamina he has, and how long you want to go on a walk. If the temperature is too hot or too cold, then you won't want to take your dog on a long walk. If it's too hot, make sure that you keep a lot of water on you. A dehydrated puppy can get sick.

Puppies have different stamina based on their breeds. If they have fat bodies or shot legs, then they're not going to be able to walk as long or as far. If you have a bigger breed that's known for their endurance, then an hour's walk may be right up their alley. You should read up on your dog breed to know how long your walks should be. Distance is up to you since you're the leader, but don't forget to keep his stamina as the weather in mind.

Crossing Roads

You don't want your puppy to be so excited that he crosses the road without you and gets hurt by accident. This is one reason you taught him to sit and stay. It's important to ask him to sit and stay at a cross road before giving him the walk command. This is important even if your puppy is on a leash. Puppies do sometimes get off leashes, and it will decrease the chance of him getting hurt by a car if he knows to sit and wait at a crossing. This process is slow, especially with how excited he is when he's out, so make sure that you're willing to put in the time and effort.

Chapter 8: Behavior Training for Puppies

If you're a puppy dog, you feel like the entire world has been created for you to enjoy. You want to play and run and bark and jump and bite. In order for puppies to become well-behaved household pets, they need to be trained in what acceptable behavior is and what isn't. While it might be fun to watch your puppy acting cute - it's not fun to listen to barking, pick up scraps of what was once your favorite pair of slippers or repair the once-landscaped backyard that has been dug to pieces. Behavior training for your puppy is absolutely necessary, for your peace of mind and your little dog's own protection.

Chewing

Chewing is a behavior that comes naturally to dogs, however it is also one that can cause a lot of damage. Puppies usually begin chewing because they explore the world with their mouths. However, they need to understand what is acceptable to chew on and what is off limits, because if they chew on the wrong thing, they can cost their owners a lot of money, and may even cost them their lives.

It is also important to understand that a puppy will chew more when he is teething, because this is a very painful process and chewing gives him some relief from the pain. If a puppy chews on inappropriate items, it is most likely to happen while he is teething. If chewing is not controlled during this time, it can become a habit that is very difficult to break later on.

The first thing you should do when teaching your puppy not to chew on inappropriate items is to make sure there are no underlying medical conditions causing the puppy to chew. There are specific dietary issues, parasites, and intestinal problems that can be the cause of this.

The next step is to puppy proof your house. Look around your house to make sure your puppy does not have access to anything that might put his life in danger. Make sure all of the household chemicals are put up and away from the puppy, and that all of the power cords are covered so the puppy cannot get to them. Remove any objects the puppy might find interesting; such as, socks or shoes.

It is best if you restrict the puppy to a small area in the home, such as the living room. This can be done using baby gates on the doorways inside of the living room. It will also make it easier on you when it comes to keeping the puppy from getting into things he shouldn't.

Give your puppy items that are okay for him to chew on. Each dog will have a different preference when it comes to what they like, so it is a good idea to provide him with a few different toys of different textures. Be careful with rawhide and beef bones because the puppy can chew on these until a small piece breaks off that could fit in the puppy's mouth and could cause him to choke.

Make sure the toys you provide for your puppy are of the appropriate size. It is important that the dog is able to pick the toy up easily and carry it around. However, it needs to be big enough that he will not swallow it. If you purchase a toy that has any type of hole in it, make sure the hole is not big enough for the dog to get his jaw stuck in it.

Do not give your puppy toys that look like items you don't want him to chew on. For example, many owners purchase a toy that looks like a shoe, while telling the dog not to chew on shoes. You should also avoid giving the dog an old shoe to chew on if you hope to teach him to not chew on new shoes.

By providing the puppy with items that he is allowed to chew, and keeping inappropriate items out of his reach, you are going to make a lot of progress when it comes to ensure that he does not wrap his teeth around anything inappropriate.

If you find the dog chewing on an item he should not be chewing on, it is important to take the item away from him and state in a loud voice, "NO." Put the item away so that he understands he is not supposed to chew on it. After you have taken the item away from the puppy, you redirect his attention by providing him with one of the toys he is allowed to chew on.

Always make sure you praise the puppy for chewing on appropriate items to ensure he learns what he should and should not chew on. If you find the puppy is having a hard time understanding which items he should not chew on, spray the item with Bitter Apple as a deterrent. If an item tastes bitter, the dog is less likely to chew on it.

You should also make sure your dog is getting enough exercise. A bored dog is likely to search for items on which he can chew. Be sure to spend time each day taking your puppy for walks, playing with him, and just spending time together. Not only will this make the bond between the two of you stronger, but it will also ensure the puppy does not destroy items that are important to you.

Barking

The next behavior to get under control is barking. Dogs bark for a variety of reasons. Most owners eventually learn what each of their dog's barks means. For example, a dog may bark in a specific way if he needs to go outside, he will bark differently if he needs food or water, and he will bark in another way if he wants to play.

Dogs also bark to warn other animals to stay away, to sound an alarm warning their owner of danger, or just because they want to bark.

Of course, you don't want to stop your puppy from every kind of barking. It is best to make sure the dog is able to warn you of danger or scare off anyone or anything that could harm you, but stop it from barking over you when you are talking, or while you are sleeping at night.

Your aim should be to stop the puppy from barking when there is no reason for him to bark. Many people make the huge mistake of paying attention to the dog when it barks, or tell it to be quiet in a loud voice, which makes the dog think you are proud of his barking, and to him, you are joining in with the barking as you 'bark' loud commands for him to be quiet.

In order to get your puppy's barking under control, you must first get to know the dog so you can begin to understand what situations might cause him to bark. When you understand why he barks, you will be able to take control of the situation and show the dog you are a confident leader for him to follow.

From the moment that you get the dog you have to begin building a strong bond with him. He has to be able to trust you and know you will take control of any situation.

There are several different ways for you to control unnecessary barking. Some people recommend holding the dog's mouth gently closed when he is barking. This is not the best way to teach your dog not to bark. Other people think you should keep the dog's mouth busy with a toy, however, you must be careful if you use this approach, because the dog may think he is being rewarded for the barking behavior.

It is important for you to teach your puppy the "quiet" command. Consistently say "quiet" in a firm and calm voice when you want him to stop barking. After he stops barking, reward him with praise and a treat. After he has mastered the command, begin giving treats less and less often until you no longer provide treats for this behavior.

Some barking can be ignored. Expect some barking when you first crate train a puppy, because he's getting used to his surroundings and will try to do whatever he can to get you to take him out of the crate. The barking will cease with time, and can be ignored for the most part.

The barking you should not ignore is when the dog barks for the sake of barking. Barking in and of itself can be rewarding for the dog, as he is having fun, and if you allow him to continue, he will think it is okay.

When you take the dog outside, be sure not to allow him to bark at those that are passing by, or to run the fence line, chasing cars as they pass by. When you show the dog you are the one in control of his behavior, he will accept that you decide when and where he can bark.

Biting

There are many reasons why dogs become aggressive and bite. The dog may feel overexcited or threatened. A lot of dog aggression comes from the lack of confidence and positive training. It is important that you socialize your dog with different people, dogs, children, and environments. Socialization will boost his confidence and reduce his fear in new environments.

Teaching a dog not to bite is vital. Most people do not enjoy playing with a dog that is known for mouthing, chewing, or biting on hands, clothing, or other body parts. It is important for you to get this type of behavior under control early on, because as the puppy gets older, it is much less likely he will be sensitive to your reaction when he bites. It is likely that an adult dog who bites or chews on people was not taught to be gentle when he was a puppy.

Mouthing is a natural behavior for dogs, because they explore the world with their mouths. Biting, on the other hand, is a reaction to either fear or frustration.

It is important for you to be able to tell the difference between playful mouthing and aggressive biting. You see, most people enjoy wrestling with their dogs, and they have no problem placing their hands in the dogs' mouths, which helps to build trust between the people and their dogs. It is important for owners to know that their dogs are not going to viciously bite them. When a dog is play mouthing, the dog's body will be relaxed, his tail will wag, and although his face may be wrinkled, it is obvious from his behavior that he is not being aggressive.

An angry or frightened dog, on the other hand, will have a stiff body, his muscles will be tense, and his tail will be straight. Most of the time, the dog will mouth a person before the bite as a warning, but this is not always the case.

If you want to teach your puppy not to bite or mouth your body parts or clothing, spend some time playing with him. Allow the puppy to mouth your hand as you play, but as soon as he does, let out a yelp as if the puppy has seriously hurt you, and allow your hand to go limp, startling your dog.

This should immediately stop the puppy from mouthing your hand. Praise the dog for stopping. Often times you will find that the dog will lick your hand. Resume play, and repeat the process if the dog mouths you again. Play with your pup for about 15 minutes. Continue to do this every day until the dog no longer mouths you.

Mouthing is another reason why it is important to provide your dog with a wide variety of chew toys of different textures. When the puppy has the toys, he is much less likely to bite during play time.

Digging

Some dogs will turn their owner's yards upside down, making the owner feel as if they are doing it all on purpose. However, dogs dig for a variety of reasons, none of them being to get revenge on their owners. Dogs dig because they are bored, seeking attention, hunting prey, entertaining themselves, or seeking protection, to name a few reasons.

The first thing to do if you want to stop your puppy from digging is to find out why the dog is digging in the first place. If the dog is left alone and outside for long periods of time with no one to keep him company, he may begin digging. In this case, ensure that you go outside and play with him. It is also a good idea to ensure that he has plenty of toys to play with. Make sure you are walking the dog at least twice each day, in order to guarantee he is getting enough exercise and stimulation.

If your puppy is digging for prey, it will most likely be near the roots of trees. You can take steps to fence the animal out, or use humane ways to catch the animal and move it to a safer place. However, you should never use poison of any type, because the poison can also hurt or kill your puppy.

Dogs will dig large holes to lay in if they are left outside in hot weather, or to shield themselves from the cold, wind, or rain. This means the dog is searching for comfort, as well as protection. In order to prevent this, make sure your puppy has adequate shelter while he is outside. You can also bring the dog inside more often, in order to protect him from extreme weather.

Make sure that the dog has a full bowl of water, and that there is no way for the bowl to flip over. If the dog prefers to lay in a hole in the ground, make sure he has an area in the yard where he is allowed to dig.

A dog may also dig as a way to get attention. Often times this happens when the dog does not get enough time with, or attention from, the owner. The only way to stop this type of behavior is to provide the dog with the love and attention he deserves.

Dogs also dig as a way to escape. This can occur if the dog is trying to get something outside of the pen, or if he is trying to get away from something. The first thing you need to do is figure out if he is trying to get to something outside of the pen, and remove the item from his view. The next thing you need to do is to make sure the pen is inviting and appealing to your dog.

You also need to think about your home as well. If the environment is stressful to the puppy, he may try to dig under the fence to get away. If there is a lot of yelling, arguing, and stress in the home, the dog will feel it, and he won't be comfortable there. Make sure you do your best to provide your puppy with a safe and loving environment so he will not want to run away.

You can bury chicken wire under the fencing of the dog's pen, but make sure that any sharp edges are turned outwards and away from the puppy. You can also place large rocks that have been partially buried at the bottom of the fence.

You should not, however, punish the puppy after he has been digging, because this will only cause him to feel more anxiety and make him want to get away.

Behavior training for puppies might seem overwhelming, but if you follow these tips, you'll have a well-behaved dog in no time.

Conclusion

If you want to raise your puppy into a good dog who knows what is expected, then you need to train him. Always be in the right mindset, and be willing to pick up training at another time if things start to get out of control. Each puppy learns at a different pace, so you have to work with your puppy. Start your training right away and don't give up until you have the behaviors you want from your puppy.

Finally, I want to thank you for reading my book. If you enjoyed the book, please take the time to share your thoughts and post a review on the <u>Puppy Training: A Step-by-Step Guide to Crate Training, Potty Training, and Obedience Training</u> Amazon book page. It would be greatly appreciated!

Best wishes,

Alexa Parsons

Check Out My Other Books

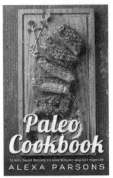

Paleo Cookbook: 52 Best Paleo Recipes to Lose Weight and Get Healthy
https://www.amazon.com/Paleo-Cookbook-Recipes-Weight-Healthy-ebook/dp/B0773Z486V/

Heart Health: 20 Healthy Habits to Prevent and Reverse Heart Disease
https://www.amazon.com/dp/B073ZQL6KL/

Diabetes: 15 Healthy Habits to Lower Blood Sugar Naturally
https://www.amazon.com/dp/B073ZP7JZC/

Running: How to Start Running to Lose Weight and Get Fit
https://www.amazon.com/dp/B073ZGCGQ4/

Pregnancy: Your Week-by-Week Guide to a Healthy Pregnancy
https://www.amazon.com/Pregnancy-Week-Week-Guide-Healthy-ebook/dp/B074JPPC87/

Made in the USA
Lexington, KY
28 March 2019